DOGFIGHT
JET FIGHTERS IN COMBAT

DOGFIGHT
JET FIGHTERS IN COMBAT

Chris Allan

Osprey Colour Series

Contents

Published in 1989 by Osprey Publishing
Limited
59 Grosvenor Street, London W1X 9DA

British Library Cataloguing in Publication
Data
Allan, Chris, 1956–
    Dogfight: jet fighters in combat
    1. Jet fighter aeroplanes –
    Illustrations
    I. Title
    623.74'63

ISBN 0-85045-866-8

Editor Dennis Baldry
Designed by Martin Richards
Printed in Hong Kong

Front cover Self-portrait of a 'scopie', perhaps better known as a RIO (Radar Intercept Officer), in the back seat of a Grumman F-14A Tomcat operated by the US Navy squadron VF-101 'Grim Reapers'. As the East Coast RAG (Replacement Air Group), all F-14 pilots and RIOs train on type with the 'Reapers' at Oceana, Virginia, before progressing to a Fleet squadron

Title pages Eagle dawn: I took this shot of a lineup of visiting F-15s from the 32nd Tactical Fighter Squadron, US Air Force, as I began my 'rounds' as duty pilot at RAF Binbrook that day. Shortly afterwards, I went on to check the condition of the runway's surface before the first sorties of the day were launched

Right The RAF's two squadrons of Buccaneer maritime strike aircraft usually try to avoid interception, but that doesn't mean they won't 'have a go' at fighters if the opportunity arises. It helps if the Buccaneer has something to shoot back with of course, and (unlike this example) a number of Buccaneers in each strike package will be armed with Sidewinders. Had plans to fit the Buccaneer with a gunpack not been cancelled to save money, the pilot of this machine would have been able to do more than shake his fist at me!

Back cover GRIZZO (left) and SWEATER, two F-16 pilots from No 323 Sqn, Royal Netherlands Air Force, relive an engagement by talking with their hands, a practice which is as old as fighter aviation

Acknowledgements

Majs Ammie, Kaufold and Wisdom
  of the 527th Aggressor Sqn
Zoë Bolsover
Sqn Ldr Simon Bryant
Sqn Ldr Tony Burtenshaw
Wg Cdr Edwards
Lt Col Hanlin
Capt John Hayden
Sqn Ldr Ian Howe
Canon UK Ltd
Wg Cdr Jake Jarron
Sqn Ldr John McGarry
The Red Arrows, especially team
  leader Sqn Ldr Tim Miller
Maj Sam Shiver, ANG
Sqn Ldr Nigel Tuffs

Sqn Ldr John McGarry, an RAF exchange pilot with VF-101 at Oceana, demonstrates some of the finer points of air combat with models of the Kfir (top) and F/A-18 Hornet for the benefit of *ab initio* students

Introduction

About the author

This book is not an air combat manual, but an attempt to capture the excitement of visual air combat through the medium of still photography. Those who wish to pursue the subject of air combat tactics after studying the next 120 pages could do a lot worse than seek out the 'bible': *FIGHTER COMBAT: THE ART AND SCIENCE OF AIR-TO-AIR COMBAT,* written by veteran F-4 and F-14 pilot Robert L Shaw. First published in the USA in 1985, the book is also available in the UK from Patrick Stephens Ltd.

None of the engagements featured in *DOGFIGHT* are 'for real'; so you won't find any duels over the Yalu River, Hanoi, Sinai Desert or the Bekaa Valley illustrated here. Real or not, the adrenalin still flows freely when you get a tally on the 'bad guy', kick in the afterburners, and go after him, if necessary pulling as much G as you can handle to get into missile launch parameters or close enough to go for guns. If the bad guy slides into *your* six o'clock, the adrenalin count goes straight through the canopy!

DOGFIGHT was photographed during the course of normal training flights in the UK and USA using hand-held cameras, or a camera pod of the author's own design. Canon, Nikon and Rolleiflex camera equipment was used, loaded with Fuji and Kodachrome film. The views expressed in this book are the author's and do not necessarily reflect those of the Ministry of Defence or of the Royal Air Force.

The Osprey Colour Series' books *FAST JETS: A pilot's eye view*, and the follow-up, *FAST JETS 2*, have established Chris Allan as one of the world's foremost aviation photographers.

After eleven years in the Royal Air Force, where he had the distinction of being the last RAF pilot to qualify on the Folland Gnat trainer, and achieved over 1500 hr on the now-retired Lightning interceptor, he decided to leave the service to pursue a career in civil aviation.

He made his 'last flight as captain' in a Lightning F.6 on 22 August 1987, during the course of the last Binbrook Open Day. His Mach 0.98 low-level flyby will be remembered by everyone who saw it on that decidedly damp summer's afternoon, his Lightning virtually disappearing in a cloud of transonic vapour.

Chris Allan is currently based in Kowloon, Hong Kong, where he serves as a First Officer on the Boeing 747-400 with Cathay Pacific Airways Limited. He does, however, remain an officer in the RAF Volunteer Reserve (VR).

Admirers of his work will be happy to know that he has set up the Chris Allan Aviation Library, which offers a regularly updated range of colour photographic transparencies on civil and military subjects. Enquiries should be addressed to the Chris Allan Aviation Library, 21–22 St Albans Place, Upper Street, London N1.

F-16: The Ultimate Dogfighter?

Left The 125th FIG (Fighter Interceptor Group) of the Florida Air National Guard converted from the Convair F-106 Delta Dart between January and March 1987, and was the first US F-16 unit to be declared 100% air-to-air. Two F-16 Falcons are maintained on round-the-clock alert at the unit's Jacksonville base (and at Homestead, Miami) to counter a possible MiG threat from Cuba. The 125th FIG's fleet of F-16A/Bs are usually armed with 2 × Sidewinder AIM-9L/M infrared-guided missiles when standing alert, although the aircraft is capable of carrying another pair if required. Pilots are so taken aback by the F-16's manoeuvring capabilities that a Chinese philosopher, one Wow F**k, is reputed to sit on their shoulders for up to the first 100 hours on type

Below It isn't easy to maintain your lookout and all-important situational awareness in a 9G turn. Florida Falcon pilots work out using this head and neck exercising equipment to help them withstand the stresses of sustained high-G manoeuvring

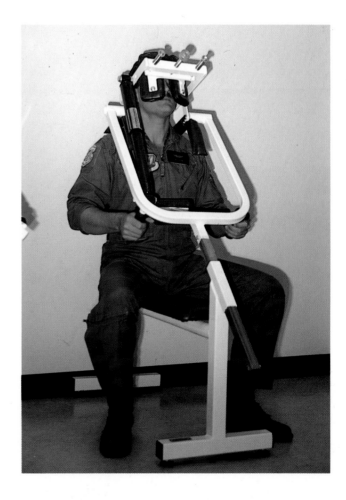

Left When it comes to presentation and professionalism, few military units can match the 'weekend warriors' of the Air National Guard. This immaculate brain bucket belongs to an F-16 pilot of the 159th FIS (Fighter Interceptor Squadron) of the 125th FIG, Florida ANG

Below If you can figure out this 405th Tactical Training Wing patch, you'll probably do well on Luke's Air Combat Manoeuvring Range

Main picture The main computer/monitoring station at Luke's ACMI range, watched by a computer technician (right) and a qualified F-15 pilot. The left screen displays the 'play area', which is located near the Mexican border, and shows the geographic orientation of the fight. The right screen displays all the information required to monitor each aircraft's progress and combat performance during the engagement (see below). The F-15 pilot is there to assess the validity of claims and ensure that range safety rules aren't violated

Below left The information displayed on the right screen includes aircraft altitude, bearing, Mach number, indicated airspeed (IAS), altitude, angle-of-attack (AOA) and G-loading. This is a 2 v 2 engagement, as indicated by the green presentation of A/C's 1 and 2, and the red presentation of A/C's 3 and 4

Top, inset A time-lapsed presentation at the post-merge phase of a fight between A/C's 3 and 2. A/C 3 has achieved a confirmed Sidewinder AIM-9L missile kill on A/C 2, hence the green coffin symbol surrounding his hapless victim. Unfortunately, A/C 3 has wasted his second Sidewinder (indicated by the green line) by launching it against the same target. Result? A potentially embarrassing overkill

Far left Ground controllers and staff pilots can select any cockpit view as required to observe each aircraft's spatial orientation. A/C 1 has claimed a 9L kill. The line slashing across the screen is the horizon

13

A fish-eye view from the rear cockpit of an F-16B, which has the same combat capability as its single-seat stablemate

Right Another view from your trainee GIB ('Guy In Back') in the F-16B's rear seat, this time looking forward. Canopy glare and internal reflections are major problems when it comes to obtaining early visual acquisition of the target

Below 'Checking Six'—probably the oldest and most important of air combat maxims—is an easy operation in the F-16

This page An F-16A of the 125th FIS cruises above its native Florida. In common with other pilots converting fom conventional fighters, the ex-Delta Dart drivers of the Florida ANG had to adjust their air combat tactics in order to exploit the F-16's amazing turn rate. This capability is demonstrated by the 'turn rate' achieved by flicking your wrist (= F-16), as compared to the roll of the hand when you bend at the elbow (= F-4, F-106, etc). This 'flickability' enables an F-16 pilot to arrive at the 'control zone' behind the bogie—the aim of an offensive Basic Fighter Manoeuvre (BFM)—from where he 'drives' the fight and from where his opponent, because of the F-16's superior manoeuvring capability, cannot dislodge him. The control zone is what you aim for once you have entered the bogie's turn circle, and varies according to your missile capability. You bid for position in the control zone by using your G-capability and out-rating him. In the control zone, you are the puppet master, and he the marionnette. . .

Overleaf SWAMP FOX versus FANG, round one! An attempt to pull into our six o'clock position results in a classic rolling scissors, where each aircraft tries to get the other to overshoot. The fight degenerates into the low speed regime until, at 150 knots, 'he's in the phone booth'
Overleaf, inset Rolling in over the top—an offensive manoeuvre
The next four pages In converting kinetic to potential energy by looping, the pilot can re-commit himself to the fight by pulling back into the merge. In coming down to the vertical, the pilot has the ability to roll into a different plane of engagement as required. Keeping the fight in the vertical plane gives the pilot more manoeuvring options, but it can also leave his fighter dangerously slow and vulnerable to missile attack from below, particularly if the missile happens to be radar guided and is emerging from ground clutter

Left Rolled out in the vertical with manoeuvre flap deployed

Above Airbrakes extended, an F-16B of the 58th TFW (Tactical Fighter Wing) touches down at Luke AFB in Arizona

Inset The rear cockpit of the F-16B is dominated by a large CRT screen, which displays information from the radar, head-up display and radar warning receiver as required. The digital weapons status panel at bottom left informs us that our two Sidewinder AIM-9L missiles are cool (ready)

Far left An attack from out of the sun remains a viable air combat tactic. The sun can also be used defensively to minimize the threat from infrared-guided missiles

Top Reefing in for guns. The F-16's built-in armament is the familiar M61A1 20 mm six-barrel cannon. For the record, the difference between machine guns and cannon lies in the type of ammunition used. Machine guns fire metal cased bullets, whereas cannon employ shells fitted with rotating rings

Bottom G-grunt. Vapour trails may be exciting to watch at air displays, but in combat they are a tell-tale sign of hard manoeuvring. The pilot of this F-16 is doing his best to try and pull the sight onto the target

Main picture In a daylight visual environment good lookout is essential, especially against a threat with his radar switched off and therefore undetected by your RWR

Far right The threat sighted, manoeuvre flap is selected as we enter a high-G, slow speed fight—the almost inevitable result of a combat between two F-16s. One has to revert to basic fighter manoeuvres against a like type

Above An F-16A of No 323 Sqn, Royal Netherlands Air Force, displays the aircraft's typical combat configuration of two Sidewinders and a centreline tank—and a 'zap' courtesy of No 43 Sqn, 'The Fighting Cocks', on the nearest ventral strake. No 43, the first RAF squadron to fly the Phantom in the air defence role, have operated the F-4K version from their base at Leuchars, Scotland, for the past 20 years

Fox One

Far left The Panavia Tornado F.3 interceptor will form the bulk of the RAF's air defence force until well into the next century. Streaming vapour from its wing tips, this pristine example from No 29 Sqn is armed with four Sky Flash medium range radar-guided missiles under the belly (these are drill rounds, identified by the blue circles painted on the forward fins) and two (with provision for four) Sidewinder AIM-9L IR-guided missiles underwing. The heart of the weapons system is its AI.24 Foxhunter pulse-Doppler radar, which the navigator manipulates to guide the Sky Flash missiles, leaving the pilot to handle the Sidewinders and the aircraft's single Mauser 27 mm cannon

Below A 'clean' (aerodynamically, that is) Tornado F.2 from No 229 Operational Conversion Unit, which trains all Tornado air defence crews on type at RAF Coningsby in Lincolnshire. The aircraft's dirty fin is a result of the muck thrown up when the thrust-reverser buckets are deployed on landing

After rejecting the F-15 Eagle and F-14 Tomcat on the grounds of cost and operational unsuitability, the RAF decided to order the Tornado ADV (Air Defence Variant), a development of the IDS (Interdictor/Strike) version, to fulfill its unique requirement for an interceptor to defend the UK Air Defence Region. This task demands the capability to patrol for extended periods at the fringes of the UKADR and deal effectively with large formations of enemy aircraft at long range in a dense electronic countermeasures environment. Problems with the Foxhunter radar have bedevilled the ADV programme from before the first F.2 was delivered in March 1984, but by the spring of 1989 it looked as though the aircraft was capable of delivering a real advance in mission capability over the aged Phantom fleet. This F.3 exhibits a problem which is by no means unique to Tornado—glinting paintwork. A flash of light from your aircraft is just what you don't need when enemy fighters are on the prowl

With wings set at mid-sweep, a Tornado turns into the threat on CAP (Combat Air Patrol). The Tornado F.3 is probably the fastest fighter in the world at low-level, having being flown at speeds above 800 knots indicated during the course of flight test development

A Tornado F.3 accelerates in high-speed configuration with its wings
swept back fully at 67 degrees

Look-down/shoot-down. A Sky Flash streaks away from Tornado F.2 ZD941/AU of No 229 OCU. Interestingly, the plunger rods (clearly visible in these photos), proved too powerful during early trials and broke up the missile as it was being released into the undisturbed airstream below the fighter. The leading edges of the all-moving tailplanes are protected to prevent damage from missile exhaust

Although a superb performer at low level, the Tornado is rather less spritely at medium to high level when compared to turbojet-powered fighters such as the Lightning. However, this shortfall is compensated for by the look-up/shoot-up capability of the Foxhunter radar/Sky Flash missile. ZD904/AE is one of 18 production F.2s (including six F.2T 'twin-stickers') delivered to No 229 OCU. The RAF is expected to receive a total of 147 F.3s by the early 1990s, sufficient to equip up to seven squadrons

Fox Two

Left Help! No wonder the
Argentines dubbed the Sea Harrier
'La Muerta Negra' (The Black
Death) when, as *FLYING's* Nigel
Moll wrote, 'The Empire struck
back in the South Atlantic.' After
the Task Force set sail to liberate
the Falklands in 1982, many
armchair Air Marshals predicted
that the Royal Navy's Sea Harriers
would be massacred by Mach 2
Mirages, but the feisty 'Jump Jet'
ended the conflict with no less
than 23 confirmed kills for no
losses in air combat. As a result of
combat experience, however, the
Sea Harrier's Sidewinder armament
was doubled, and the FRS.2
version will introduce Blue Vixen
pulse-Doppler radar to engage
multiple low-level targets beyond
visual range. In common with the
Tornado F.3, the FRS.2 will be
compatible with the AIM-120
advanced radar-guided AAM

Right A more peaceful study of a
Sea Harrier FRS.1 of No 899 Naval
Air Squadron as it climbs near its
base at Yeovilton in Somerset.
Some 40 FRS.1 aircraft are
expected to be rotated through a
mid-life update programme to bring
them up to FRS.2 standards

Above Harrier versus Harrier: a view through the HUD from the rear cockpit of a Harrier T.4 operational trainer during an ACM (Air Combat Manoeuvring) exercise

Right and overleaf Harrier GR.3 firing a Sidewinder AIM-9G at a flare target towed behind a Jindivik drone

Overleaf inset Fox Two: the Sidewinder explodes close abeam the flare target. The Harrier family are the only combat aircraft which can VIFF (Vector In Forward Flight) to shake off an opponent or gain a position to take the offensive

Above A Lightning F.6 breaks away to reveal a brace of dummy Red Top missiles, carried without fins to minimize fatigue damage. The last Lightning squadron, No 11, disbanded at RAF Binbrook in Lincolnshire on 30 April 1988, but before the aircraft faded into history some of the remaining live Red Tops were fired during MPC (Missile Practice Camp) at RAF Valley the year before. No 11 Sqn has since reformed and is now mounted on the Tornado F.3 at RAF Leeming in North Yorkshire

Right and overleaf 'Firing, firing, now!' A Red Top in pure pursuit towards the flare towed behind a 'Jindy' (both visible overleaf in the last photo of sequence). The Jindy is safe as long as the flare stays lit

Above and right The RAF's
Red Arrows, demonstrating bas
manoeuvres during pre-season
war, the team's Hawk T.1As w
AIM-9L Sidewinders, have thei
Aden cannon restored, and join
Britain's airfields and other key

Below High-G barrel: the offe
crossing the circle in order to c
in left-hand orbit

Above A similar situation, but this time the energy of
the offensive Hawk is not excessive and the pilot
elects to fly to the aircraft's limit (in phase) but only
slightly outside the target's flight path. End result? The
same steady solution

Left and right Classic rolling combat scissors: the
aim is to fly as slowly as possible, for as long as
possible, by barrelling around your opponent and
thereby forcing him in front. But you must be careful
not to fly too slowly, otherwise the bogey can use his
energy to nip in behind you. The skill is in knowing
when to go slow, and when to pull high whilst
maintaining your ability to manoeuvre

Left There are those who would say that the Tornado ADV and F-4 Phantom aren't the RAF's only two-seat fighters! In aggressive mood, this Hunter T.7A of No 237 OCU based at RAF Lossiemouth in Scotland seems to have forgotten that its role is to facilitate the type conversion of pilots selected to fly the Buccaneer. The Hunter T.7A is clearly a real fighter disguised as a trainer. . .

Below This Tornado F.2 navigator's eye view again demonstrates the problem of glare and internal reflections on the canopy. The bogey is about to cross our nose

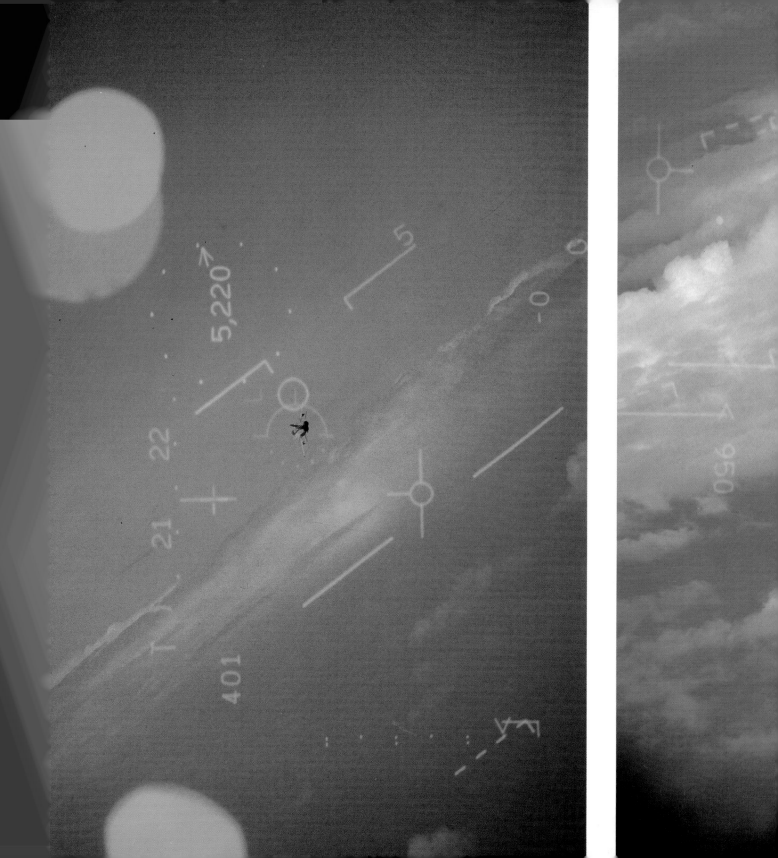

Far left The altimeter arrow (top right of photo), can move clockwise or anti-clockwise, and shows 5220 feet as the target tracks to the left. The HUD is locked to the aircraft's longitudinal fuselage datum

Left The target is rolling and pulling through a descending hard right turn. The introduction of HOTAS (Hands On Throttle And Stick) controls will enhance the ADV's operational effectiveness

Below We're heading north (true) at 328 knots/10,950 feet. When descending through 5000 feet, the radar altimeter (Radalt) takes over from the standard barometric instrument to ensure a high degree of accuracy. During the engagement, the pilot noticed the HUD was displaying a transient state of Sidewinder locked/unlocked attack because the radar was continually unlocking, so he therefore locked the Sidewinder's seeker head

The Aggressors

An aggressor driver moves in closer for a better look. The Northrop F-5E Tiger II is a sleek beast and fulfilled the role of a third generation MiG-21 or MiG-23 to perfection when flown by the 527th. To keep pace with Soviet aircraft advances the squadron retired its venerable Tiger IIs and now flies the fourth generation F-16C. The small blade aerials under the nose of the F-5E are TACAN and UHF/IFF navigation aids

Right Leaving you in no doubt as to the purpose of the 527th Aggressor Squadron (AS), the unit badge typifies the spirit of an aggressor pilot

Below The man behind the mask. Captain Scott MINGO Ahmie is an 'aggressor' in the true sense of the word, having flown the Tiger II for over three and a half years. Ahmie started his Air Force career as a 'Phabulous Phantom' pilot, serving as a 'Wild Weasel' driver with the 90th TFS at Clark AFB in the Philippines. He then went to Nellis and flew F-5E aggressors before returning to the 3rd TFW at Clark. Assigned to the 26th AS, Ahmie commenced a long working relationship with the Northrop 'rocket' and now has over 600 hr on type

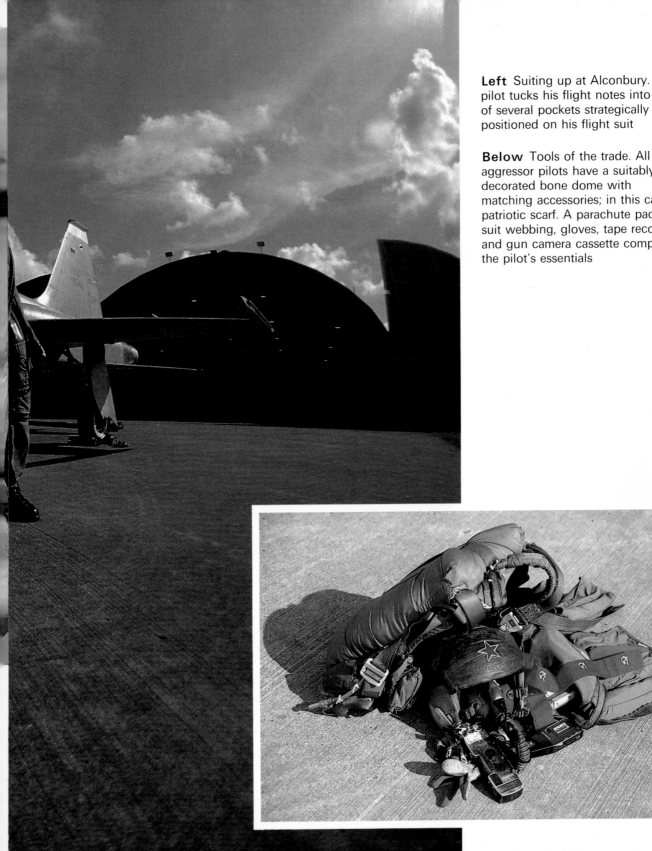

Left Suiting up at Alconbury. The pilot tucks his flight notes into one of several pockets strategically positioned on his flight suit

Below Tools of the trade. All chic aggressor pilots have a suitably decorated bone dome with matching accessories; in this case a patriotic scarf. A parachute pack, G suit webbing, gloves, tape recorder and gun camera cassette complete the pilot's essentials

The real thing. The principal reason for the 527th trading in their venerable Tiger IIs was the appearance of this aircraft in bulk with the Frontal Aviation regiments of the Soviet Air Force. The MiG-29 *Fulcrum*, along with the Sukhoi Su-27 *Flanker*, is a fourth generation Soviet fighter and the 527th AS, like the US Navy, employs the 'slippery' F-16C Fighting Falcon as its simulator

Combat at Key West

Left Usually a bustling flightline. As dusk approaches, the ramp at Key West is once again the silent domain of the squadron groundcrews working to prepare the aircraft for tomorrow's sorties

82

The opposite ends of the fighter spectrum sit parked alongside each other on the NAS Key West flightline. Although technically not a fighter, this TA-4J is used by VF-45 as a MiG-17/second generation simulator because of its low power and extreme agility

Right Another day, another dollar. F-14s of VF-101 'Grim Reapers' are marshalled out to commence the first sortie of the day. Although a flightline is not quite as congested a space as the deck of an aircraft-carrier, getting four Tomcats launched in double quick time, and in the right order is still no mean feat

One of the most unusual and arguably the most handsome of schemes ever to grace the diminutive A-4 has to be this artistic effort from the VF-45 paint shop

Left A plane captain from VF-45 looks on intently as the crew thoroughly inspect the fuel flow pump compartment on their TA-4J. The Skyhawk is neatly painted up in a South-East Asian camouflage scheme, effective over lush tropical jungles, but of questionable value over the crystal blue waters off the coast of Key West. The twin seater Skyhawk is often crewed by a PUT (pilot under training) accompanied by an IP (instructor pilot) on many adversary missions

Below Now this A-4E has definite propulsion problems! When Ed Heinemann designed the Skyhawk over 30 years ago one of the novel features he built in was the removable tail section which allows major engine maintenance to be effected with the minimum of fuss. Devoid of both its tail and its Pratt & Whitney J52-P-408, the Skyhawk from VF-45 waits rather forlornly to be put back together again

Long term Key West residents, VF-45 now also operate ten F-16Ns and two TF-16Ns alongside their venerable Skyhawks. The re-equipping of the squadron has greatly enhanced the effectiveness of the adversary training offered by the squadron to Atlantic fleet carrier units. The unit was originally commissioned as Torpedo Squadron VT-75 during World War 2 on TBM Avengers. Designated VA-45 for many years, the squadron relocated from NAS Cecil Field to Key West in March 1980. Officially attached to the Navy's Adversary Command four years later, VA-45 came under the auspices of Fighter Wing One. The squadron received its more appropriate designation of VF-45 in February 1985

Left More than routine maintenance work is performed by a 'wingless' 'Grim Reaper' at Key West. With both Pratt & Whitney TF30 turbofans buried away deeply within the Tomcat's fuselage, hinging body panels are Godsend for the hard working groundcrew. The glossy grey radome on this particular F-14 is rather unusual

One of the more exotic types employed by a Navy adversary squadron was the Israeli Aircraft Industries (IAI) Kfir C-1. Designated the F-21A and flown by VF-43 'Challengers' for four years from 1985 to 1988, the aircraft were leased at no charge to the US government by the Israelis. The Kfirs simulated MiG-21s and MiG-23s in DACT missions flown by the 'Challengers'. With the tropical Florida palms of Key West providing an unmistakable backdrop for the F-21s, a pair of VF-43 aircraft taxi in from the runway after completing a cross country from their home base, NAS Oceana, in Virginia

Left A smokey start for an F-14 on initial fire up. This is caused by stagnant JP-5 being burnt by the engine as it's spooled up

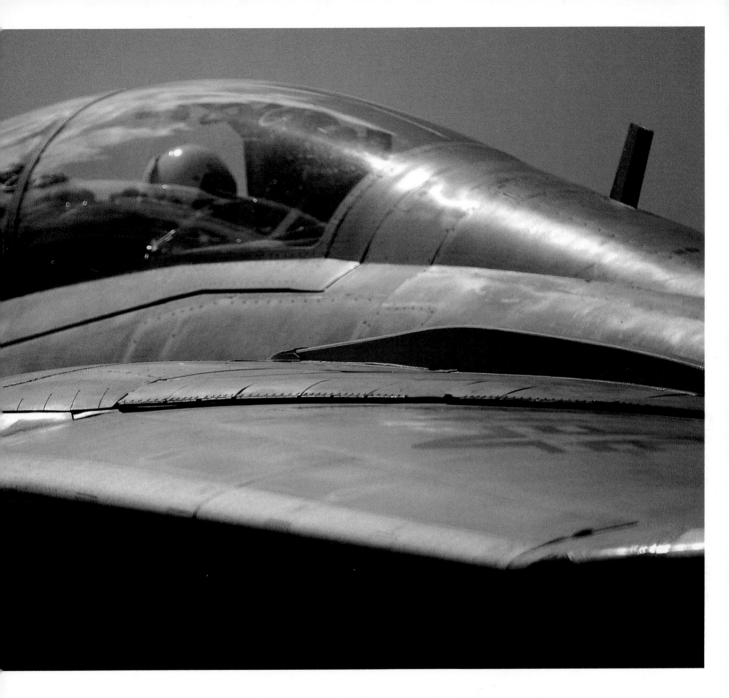

Above and following pages The styling on the Tomcat is aerodynamically brilliant, the menacing beauty of the Grumman heavyweight being shown to good effect in these close up views of the aircraft

The 'Grim Reapers' are tasked with the training of replacement aircrews and supporting other personnel destined to join Atlantic fleet Tomcat squadrons. On most missions the trainee pilot is accompanied by a seasoned radar intercept officer (RIO) instructor from the squadron, and vice versa for trainee RIOs

THIS AIRCRAFT
PYROTECHNIC-ACTUATED
ESCAPE SYSTEM
ITH EXPLOSIVE CHARGES
01-FI4AAA-2-4-3
OMPLETE INSTRUCTIONS

Above The pilot makes a quick visual check of his surroundings before easing himself into the aircraft. Vital rear vision mirrors can be seen firmly attached to the canopy framing above his head. The effective use of these mirrors is a lesson quickly learned by the potential fighter pilot when up against adversary aircraft

Left True Brit: Squadron Leader Simon Bryant, RAF, straps himself in before doing battle in the blue skies over Florida. The RAF runs a very competitive service exchange programme with the Navy, Marine Corps and Air Force

Above Being a RAG (Replacement Air Group) squadron VF-101 employs a considerable number of female sailors in the administrative and maintenance roles. The 'Reapers' are allowed to do this because they are classed as a 'non-combat' squadron who theoretically spend no longer than one to two weeks on board a carrier at a time, and should technically never see action

Left 'Let the fight begin'. A trainee pilot awaits his turn to prove his mettle in the arena of aerial combat

Below Wearing the colours of his former squadron, VF-142 'Ghostriders', on his bone dome, the RIO instructor dictates navigation details to the Key West control tower before take-off

Above Tomcat '161' taxies towards the 'last chance' check point prior to take-off. Here, VF-101 groundcrew will remove the AIM-9L Sidewinder missile safety pins from the finless training round mounted on the wing glove pylon. Although virtually an unguided projectile without its fins, the active seeker head in the Sidewinder will still track and give off a tone when it acquires a target during ACM. Most 'Grim Reaper' F-14s are now painted in drab tactical greys which contrast markedly with this glossy VF-101 Tomcat

Right 'Roger ball'. The bane of all naval aviators, the Fresnel lens system, or just simply the meatball, is the governor of modern carrier operations. The graduated lens between the lights gives the approaching pilot a smooth transition from one vertical red light to the next. The lens system is actually heated to maintain accurate beam angles. An aircraft on finals to the carrier approaches the ship in a beam 32 feet deep which stretches out to about a mile behind the vessel. The aircraft must remain roughly 16 feet either side of the beam's centre to arrive over the ship's ramp at the correct approach angle. At the carrier the maximum variation allowable is two feet. Precision flying indeed

This page and following pages Phase five afterburner propels the 60,000 lb F-14 through the heat haze on the Key West runway at a velocity approaching 160 knots. The wide spacing between the TF30s means bad news for the crew should an engine flame out during take-off or landing. Tomcats have landed with only one engine spooled up on carriers and at air stations but it's not a pleasant experience for the crew

Stealth take-off for a VF-101
Tomcat at Key West. The 'Grim
Reapers' are currently
supplementing their Tomcat ranks
with brand new F-14 Plus versions
of the Grumman fighter. The
Tomcat Plus has the same basic
fuselage as the earlier F-14 but has
General Electric F110 GE-400
engines fitted in place of the
TF30s. The new engines give the
aircraft 30 per cent more thrust in
most aspects of its flight
parameters

Above Flare and glare. The pilot pulls up and away from the author and prepares to initiate a hard 'bat turn' to port. Above the plumbing for the refuelling probe is the anti-flash shield for the twin cannons originally fitted in the wing root of the Echo model A-4, but long since removed from this Skyhawk

Opposite and following pages The beautiful Key West shoreline disappears beneath a 'Grim Reapers' F-14 as it cruises out to the ACM area many miles off the Florida coast. Originally commissioned at Cecil Field in May 1952 as part of Carrier Air Group 10 (CVG-10), VF-101 was just one of a number of units

formed to make up the numbers during the Korean War. Initially equipped with the Goodyear-built FG-1D Corsair, the unit quickly traded up to the McDonnell F2H-2 Banshee. After several cruises with the Banshee, the 'Reapers' transitioned onto the Douglas F4D-1 Skyray in 1956. In 1958 the squadron moved to Key West and became the permanent FAWTULant (Fleet All-Weather Training Unit Atlantic) squadron tasked with the training of all-weather fighter pilots. VF-101 also received Douglas F3D Skyknights and McDonnell F3H Demons to supplant their Skyrays during the merger. The first Phantom IIs reached VF-101 in June 1960 and

a special detachment was established at NAS Oceana to operate the potent new fighter, Det A later moving back to Key West in 1963. The 'Grim Reapers' finally moved their headquarters element to Oceana permanently in 1971, but a Key West det remained in Florida. The squadron began working up to become the F-14 East Coast RAG in 1975 but the last Phantom II did not leave VF-101 until 1977. Over the past twelve years the 'Reapers' have successfully transitioned eight fleet squadrons from the F-4 to the F-14, and have trained large numbers of personnel to serve with these units

As clean as they come, at least in the ordnance sense, a 'Reaper' F-14A banks away tightly from the camera ship with its wings in full sweep. During a pilot's initial combat det to Key West he works up in a 1 v 1 ACM scenario before progressing up the matrix syllabus to 1 v 2 and multi-bogey sorties

And in the blue Florida skies this is what the F-14 crew strains to get a visual fix on, though hopefully not at this distance! A bogey from VF-45 eases his A-4E in closer to the camera to get a better look

Above The training programme for a RIO is no less strenuous than that formulated for the pilot. A well trained RIO who has full spatial awareness is much more than just a paid passenger in the F-14 as his ability to professionally train the 'Mk One Eyeball' often saves their collective bacon . . .

Right This is what NAS Key West is all about. Pulling up in to the vertical the F-14 driver begins a disengaging role to starboard as he is unable to stay on the tail of the A-4 without overshooting. The

new re-engined A-4F 'Super Fox' can climb with virtually any of the fleet fighters, although the F-14 Plus would give it a run for its money

Below Unencumbered by external stores, the A-4 is virtually unbeatable in 'cheek to cheek' ACM. A pilot who can regularly knock down an adversary Skyhawk has reached the peak of his craft, the elusive fighting edge having been honed to razor sharpness

Right Looking good for a simulated three wire, an F-14 recovers after a hectic aerial brawl. Although over a mile of black top stretches out in front of the pilot all approaches on land are simulated carrier recoveries. Painted blood red, the ventral and dorsal airbrakes are clearly visible through the smokey engine exhaust

Previous page Recovery at dusk. Night landings for naval aviators are said to separate the men from the boys on the boat

Right The ultimate work place?

Last page An essential part of the pilot's survival kit! Thanks, Zoë